# Battle of
# STALINGRAD
## Russia's Great Patriotic War

Text by I.M. Baxter
Color plates by Ronald Volstad

D1288827

Editor: James R. Hill
Copyright © 2004
by CONCORD PUBLICATIONS CO.
603-609 Castle Peak Road
Kong Nam Industrial Building
10/F, B1, Tsuen Wan
New Territories, Hong Kong
www.concord-publications.com

All rights reserved. No part of
this publication may be reproduced,
stored in a retrieval system or
transmitted in any form or by any
means, electronic, mechanical,
photocopying or otherwise, without
the prior written permission of
Concord Publications Co.

We welcome authors who can help
expand our range of books. If you
would like to submit material,
please feel free to contact us.

We are always on the look-out for new,
unpublished photos for this series.
If you have photos or slides or
information you feel may be useful to
future volumes, please send them to us
for possible future publication.
Full photo credits will be given upon
publication.

ISBN 962-361-082-3
printed in Hong Kong

# Introduction

The terrain immediately surrounding the city of Stalingrad is a treeless, flat bleak steppe, which is hot and dusty in the summer and bitterly cold during the winter. By some fate, during 1942 this area covering some 60,000 square miles became the focal point for one of the most decisive battles of World War Two between Nazi Germany and Soviet Russia, involving some one million or more men, 2,000 tanks, 25,000 artillery pieces, and 2,300 aircraft.

For both the Germans and the Russians, the name of the city alone implied a personal contest between Hitler and Stalin. Hitler had made Stalingrad the goal of his grand summer offensive and would not claim success until he had captured it. Stalin felt that holding Stalingrad would give the Soviet command its last chance to demonstrate to the world that Germany was not an irrepressible foe, despite its string of victories. For both dictators, the battle at Stalingrad would decide the outcome of the war. Although the Red Army had suffered high casualties, Stalin called on every soldier and citizen alike to continue what he called the "patriotic war" and defend every brick and stone of the city until the invader had been vanquished.

The German advance on the city began on 17 July 1942, the day on which the Stalingrad Front had replaced the Southwest Front. Committed in this area were two newly created armies, the 62nd and 64th Armies, situated in the Don Bend. The forward element of both of these armies had attacked towards Rostov, driving 4.Panzer-Armee south, and leaving the overstretched and exhausted General von Paulus' 6.Armee to advance toward the city alone. By late July, 6.Armee had reported it had cleared most of the Don Bend during an impressive drive. But it suddenly ran out of steam, apparently after running low on fuel and ammunition. From south of Stalingrad, some 120 miles away, the 4.Panzer-Armee was now ordered to turn around and assist the 6.Armee in the attack on the city.

While the drive was on to reach Stalingrad, the *Stavka* (Soviet Supreme General Staff) committed the newly formed 1st and 4th Tank Armies against 6.Armee. But on 7 August 1942, the 1st Tank Army, together with the forward elements of the 62nd Army, were suddenly surprised by Paulus' troops on the west bank of the Don, and were encircled during the course of the next few days. The defeat west of Stalingrad caused consternation among the Soviet command, but they did not intend to allow their forces to repeat the same mistake inside Stalin's city. Immediately they put General Andrei Yeremenko in command of both fronts, with Nikita Khrushchev as member of the Military Council.

On 24 August 1942, the Soviet 21st, 62nd, and 1st Guards Armies attacked 6.Armee. Following two days of brutal combat and bloody attrition, the Soviet forces appeared to be breaking under the ferocious might of the Germans. It was soon reported that soldiers of the 62nd Army were falling back towards Stalingrad, enabling Paulus to strike further east to the gates of the city itself. It seemed Stalingrad was now well within his grasp.

Inside the city on 25 August, a state of siege existed, and the total evacuation of the civilian population was ordered. With the exception of a few factories remaining open for military purposes, most of the city closed down. During early September, the 62nd and 64th Armies finally withdrew into the inner defenses of Stalingrad. But on the River Volga, the 1st Guards, 24th, and 66th Armies began a counterattack against 6.Armee, blunting their advance and temporarily keeping them preoccupied for several days. In the days that followed, 6.Armee attacked into the center of Stalingrad in a bloody, relentless struggle in which single blocks and buildings became major battlefields. But despite the ferocity of the invader, the situation favored the defender, as long as he was willing to pay the price in blood.

During mid-September/early October, the 62nd Army received reinforcements, which amounted to some two tank brigades, a rifle brigade, and nine rifle divisions. A number of alterations were also made to tighten command and infuse fanatical allegiance. Yeremenko took command of Southwest Front, renamed Stalingrad Front, and General Konstantin Rokossovsky assumed command of what now became known as the Don Front.

By early October 1942, 6.Armee had effectively accomplished its objective as first set out by Hitler earlier that year. The Volga was closed and half the city was in German hands, while the rest could be razed by intensive aerial and ground bombardment. Hitler had always been concerned about wasting his soldiers in urban fighting. But now, with victory beckoning, he was determined to show Stalin his worth.

As 6.Armee continued to fight against stiff resistance, the season began changing dramatically. In early November a hard freeze set in, causing unprecedented complications in the Soviet defense lines. During the first week of November, General Vassili Chuikov's hold on the city had been reduced further to two bridgeheads, one only a mile and a half deep and the other six miles wide. But despite these set backs to the south of the city, a new developing threat was about to be unleashed against the Germans. For weeks General Georgi Zhukov, known as the defender of Russia, was building up his forces for a new massive offensive. The plan was to tie down 6.Armee on the front between the Don and

3

the Volga and in Stalingrad, smash the Romanian forces on its left, and drive with all its might behind the army to sever its lines of communications across the Don.

On 19 November 1942, the Russians finally opened up the offensive at Stalingrad. For nearly two hours hundreds of Soviet artillery pieces tore into German and Allied lines, and by daybreak the 5th Tank Army and 21st Army launched their infantry against the Romanian 3.Armee. Within hours the Romanians were brushed aside in the snow and literally battered to death. Simultaneously, the 65th Army began its attack, but it faced stiff opposition from German divisions that were not so eager to give up their front lines. South of the Beketovka bridgehead, the 51st and 57th Army broke through the Romanian IV.Armee-Korps that had disintegrated with hardly a fight. All this merged into a sudden panic flight among the allies of the Germans that consequently helped in the pending encirclement.

By 22 November, the encirclement of Stalingrad was virtually secured. Disbelief among the Germans added to the confusion. The Russians had never secured a successful breakthrough in depth. With the encirclement fully completed by the 23rd, the Russians devoted their main strength to fastening the hold on 6.Armee. By 28 November the Russians were concentrating some 94 brigades and divisions against some 49 opposing divisions that were badly equipped, under strength, exhausted, hungry, and lacking proper winter clothing.

In order to prevent any relief from reaching Stalingrad, on the Southwest Front Zhukov ordered a massive attack against the Italian Eighth and Romanian Third Army from Novaya Kalitva south of the mouth of the River Chir. Fighting in the area was fierce, and the German allies took the main brunt of the Soviet fury. By 16 December, the Soviet 6th Army broke through the Italian line east of Novaya Kalitva, almost smashing it to pieces. In the succeeding days, the 1st and 3rd Guards Armies broke through at the Don and advanced southward. By this time the temperature had dropped considerably.

By the beginning of 1943, little had been achieved by the Germans in the attempt to relieve 6.Armee. Paulus' forces were still dying a lingering death from exhaustion and starvation. Inside the ravaged city of Stalingrad, remnants of the Soviet 62nd Army were also suffering from hunger, fatigue and the harsh weather conditions. Despite the terrible conditions inside the ruins, the Germans had somewhat of a small advantage. They had some shelter and could obtain wood for fuel from demolished buildings, while the Russians had none.

During early January 1943, the Soviets resumed their offensive west of Stalingrad to further reduce the possibility of the enemy attempting a relief effort, hoping to starve 6.Armee out of existence. The strength of the Red Army during this period was very impressive. On the Don Front alone, for instance, they had almost 281,000 troops and 250 tanks. In total, there were almost 700,000 Red Army troops fighting during the battle of Stalingrad in January 1943. Given this kind of strength, the 6.Armee had no prospect of holding out, let alone breaking out of the city and surviving.

On 22 January, the Red Army moved in for the kill, which marked the beginning of the end of 6.Armee. On a wide three-mile front, marching south with battle flags unfurled, Russian troops broke through into the city and then the outer ring of the Kessel. Fighting was bitter and bloody, with the Russians incurring more losses than the defenders. But the Red Army could afford to shed more blood since there were many thousands waiting in the ranks to replace those who fell.

Despite the superiority of the Red Army, on 31 January, in the north of the Stalingrad pocket around the tractor plant, some 33,000 soldiers from 6.Korps, under General der Infanterie Karl Strecker, were still holding out. The very next day Hitler ordered this Korps to hold out to the last man. But they were already finished. They were so badly depleted and exhausted that they were unable to fight a defensive battle for long. The end had finally come.

The Germans lost some 205,000 men in the Stalingrad pocket. Some 91,000 remaining troops were captured when Paulus finally surrendered on 1 February 1943. The Soviets did not make their own losses known, but they must have been substantial. According to some unofficial figures, the losses were more than 350,000 men lost, killed and wounded. Fighting had been fierce, with the ammunition expenditure reaching unprecedented levels during the last two weeks of the battle. On the Don Front alone the Red Army used nearly one million artillery rounds of all calibers up to 203mm, nearly one million mortar shells, and multi million machine gun and rifle rounds.

Although the Russians had suffered terrible losses, the patriotic war that had first been declared in July 1941 finally yielded success. Stalin had won his battle, and the victorious cheers from Russia's Patriotic War would resound at the very gates of Berlin two years later.

All images in this book are from the Imperial War Museum, Novosti Press Agency and the HITM Archive.

General (later Marshal of the Soviet Union) Georgi Zhukov studies a map while conferring with his commanders. Zhukov was a commander of fierce determination and overwhelming strength of character. At the end of August 1942, with General Paulus' 6.Armee at the gates of Stalingrad, Zhukov was appointed Deputy Supreme Commander of the Red Army. Zhukov was given the demanding task of flying down to the burning city of Stalingrad to co-ordinate the attack of the 1st Guards Army, which was being transferred to the Stalingrad Front to slice through the German corridor from the north and join up with the 62nd Army.

On the move to Stalingrad in late August 1942, men of the 62nd Army push forward to aid their comrades in and around the besieged city. The soldiers are being transported in US-supplied vehicles, the 1/4-ton 4x4 Command Reconnaissance (Willys MA) Jeep. The Red Army received the majority of the 1500 of these vehicles that were built.

These soldiers of the 62nd Army are armed with M1891/30 Mosin Nagant rifles and PPSh-41 submachine guns. They are wearing the basic kit of a Soviet soldier, including a greatcoat or blanket with haversack, entrenching tool, and a rolled ground sheet slung across their shoulders.

Several Russian officers are driven to the front lines in a Willys MA Jeep. The local civilians of the town wish them luck and decorate the commanders with flowers. Unity among the Russian people and the Red Army was brought together by a war that Stalin had characterized in July 1941 as a "patriotic war."

An officer addresses members of one of the Russian mechanized units, some of whom appear to be female. Note their padded tanker helmets.

At the Stalingrad Front a motorcycle reconnaissance unit patrols the vast steppes before the Volga in late August1942. Note how foliage has been attached to the vehicles. The soldiers sitting in the sidecars are armed with PPSh-41 submachine guns.

A group of Red Army troops who have crossed a river haul a Maxim 1910 water-cooled machine gun up an embankment. The machine gun is on its wheeled Sokolov mount, of which the shield alone weighs a staggering 74kg (163lb). Note the soldier carrying two ammunition boxes.

Just like the German army they opposed, the Red Army made widespread use of horses for transportation purposes during the Great Patriotic War.

The Red army made use of a variety of artillery ranging from mortars to howitzers, like this 76mm anti-tank gun, to defend the "Motherland" from the invading German forces.

Russian troops push a 45mm (1.77in) Model 1932 L/46 gun down a road while an officer carrying field glasses signals to unseen soldiers behind the cameraman.

A Russian M1931 203mm howitzer is being loaded for action. A well-trained crew was able to keep up fire for many hours, despite its crude design. The Red Army used the howitzer widely on the Eastern Front. Firing a 98.5kg (217lb) shell, it was an especially effective weapon when used against immobile targets such as German strongpoints and when defending buildings.

German soldiers examine an abandoned Russian truck, which has a mounted quad 7.62mm Pulemet Maksima Obrazets 1910 Maxim machine gun. The firing rate of this old weapon was between 2,080 to 2,400 rounds per minute. This weapon was used mainly in an anti-aircraft role, but was also effective against mobile infantry.

Dressed in summer uniforms, including *pilotka* sidecaps, Soviet troops make slow progress in an advance against the German invaders. The soldiers at left are hauling a Maxim 1910 machine gun toward the front lines.

Soldiers from the 62nd Army in late August 1942. Although this propaganda picture depicts Red Army soldiers victoriously forging ahead against the "Nazi invader", they are more likely withdrawing from leading elements of 6.Armee. All the men are armed with the ubiquitous PPSh-41 submachine gun and are wearing the basic summer kit.

Soldiers of the 62nd Army advance after beating back enemy resistance in a populated area. Although this picture depicts the Red Army as victors, they were actually already cut off in the north by 6.Armee.

Attempting to stem the German onslaught on Stalingrad. Although this photograph appears to show Soviet soldiers advancing, they are more likely being compressed by fierce enemy attacks and are on the defensive. In an attempt to go unnoticed in the vast open spaces, several soldiers have attached foliage to their kit and steel helmets for added camouflage protection. One of the troops appears to be armed with a captured Italian Fucile Mitriagliatori Breda Modello 30. This weapon was an air-cooled machine gun that fired between 450 and 500 rpm.

Soviet soldiers moving forward toward Stalingrad. All of the men are armed with PPSh-41 submachine guns and wear ankle boots. Their legs are wrapped in puttees made from cloth from worn-out uniforms. The soldiers are more than likely on patrol in this region. Within weeks of this photograph being taken, the iron ring around Stalingrad had been closed.

Soldiers rush forward through smoke and dirt that blackens the air around them. One of them is carrying a 14.5mm PTRS M1941 anti-tank gun.

Unwilling to give a yard of ground without shedding enemy blood, Russian soldiers try to hold their positions to the last man. Here Russian infantrymen keep low as they endure steady German attacks. Behind the soldier armed with a PPSh-41 submachine gun, three of his comrades hold 7.62mm Samozariadnyia Vintovka Tokareva o1940g, or SVT-40 automatic rifles.

Russian gunners return fire with a 45mm Model 1932 L/46 infantry gun in support of advancing Soviet troops.

Reserves from the Red Army are seen on their way to the front lines. This regiment is crossing a water barrier in the Stalingrad area. Because the rivers were so wide, only long-range artillery could hit positions on the far bank. German gunners would register riverbanks as targets for fire missions because Russian soldiers would concentrate there before crossing.

Captured Russian soldiers, who were photographed in front of Stalingrad during late August 1942. These infantrymen are probably part of the 62nd Army.

Stalin regarded soldiers who surrendered, such as these men, as traitors.

Trucks laden with troops are seen moving to the front in August 1942. The troops are wearing the basic kit of a Soviet soldier. The men are armed with Mosin Nagant Model 1891/30 rifles that weighed 4kg (8.8lb) empty and had a muzzle velocity of 811m/s (2,661ft/s). Although it was an old weapon, it was very effective and reliable.

These Russian troops, who probably belong to the 62nd Army, were captured by units from General Paulus' 6.Armee. The fate of these Soviet prisoners is unknown. On the seemingly endless expanses of flat plains and fertile steppes shown here, a bloodlust of unrivalled proportions was born. Already, by the late summer of 1942, millions of Russian soldiers and civilians had perished in a war of hatred and barbarism. Although the Red Army suffered high casualties, their devotion to the "Motherland" and their courageous determination to halt the German crusade continued on with violent fanaticism.

Russian troops advance under fire on the Stalingrad Front. In the distance a T-34/76 tank moves at speed to achieve its first tactical objective. A common Soviet tactic was to allow the infantry to ride close to the German positions, clinging onto the sides of the tank, to help them destroy enemy anti-tank positions before the tanks made the breakthrough. However, this tactic normally resulted in unprecedented casualties since the German machine guns often cut down the troops before they had time to reach their objective. On many occasions the soldiers would get deliberately intoxicated on Vodka before being sent screaming into battle against German positions.

Under intensive artillery fire from superior German positions, three Russian soldiers crawl forward while shells pounds the area ahead of them. Many Russian soldiers were astounded at the speed of the German advance on Stalingrad and the sudden collapse of their own army. Yeremenko had sent his forces north to meet *panzers* from 6.Armee coming from the river Volga, but the battering ram of Paulus' army was too strong for him to affect the situation decisively.

Soviet soldiers creep forward against a selected target as part of a localized counterattack during the German advance into the Stalingrad area. Red Army troops were ordered to attack a multitude of targets, especially when it would cause inconvenience to the enemy, such as destroying bridges. Although attacks on bridges hindered the German advance and reduced their mobility considerably, they also caused problems for the local population.

Red Army soldiers advance through a settlement near Stalingrad in another attempt to eliminate a German strongpoint. They are all armed with PPSh-41 submachine guns. Of interest are the camouflaged steel helmets. Foliage is held in place on the helmets by means of chicken wire. The chicken wire was shaped over the helmets and set into position using three or four crude hooks. This allowed the wearer to add foliage, grass and even twigs over the entire helmet.

Positioned along a newly dug trench, members of a Soviet assault squad fire their PPSh-41 machine guns across open terrain. This photograph appears to be carefully posed since the PPSh-41 fired a 7.62mm (0.3in) pistol-caliber round that was not very effective against distant targets. The weapon had a simple short-range flip sight that was more accurate and deadly in close quarter battle or urban combat, such as in Stalingrad. Two of the machine gunners are dressed in *vatnaya telogreika* or padded jackets.

Two officers, the one on the right armed with a PPSh-41 submachine gun, receive reconnaissance reports from a motorcycle dispatch rider. With the Stalingrad Front fluctuating, constant reconnaissance reports were an absolute necessity. The battle of Stalingrad was fought across some 96,540 square kilometers (60,000 square miles) of battlefield. It was, therefore, vital for the commanders to know the location and strength of the enemy.

Troops and horse-drawn transports are being ferried across the Volga on inflatable boats. Supplying Stalingrad was vital, but crossing the Volga was often extremely dangerous and deadly. Providing no cover, the large expanse of water was very daunting for soldiers. Hundreds of troops fell victim to enemy air attacks and the heavy artillery bombardment of the river. Although shells might not score direct hits, the waves from a large explosion were sometimes sufficient to make an overcrowded raft or boat unstable. If a shell or a sniper's bullet did not kill you, there was still the prospect of drowning.

A happy welcome. Peasant women rejoice at the recapture of a village northwest of the city and embrace their young patriotic warriors.

A spectacular photograph showing a battery of 132mm (5.20in) *Katyusha* or Little Katy M13 16-rail rocket launchers firing 42.5kg (93.6lb) rockets into German-held positions. These were fired from converted US Studebaker 6x4 $2\frac{1}{2}$-ton trucks. The first of these rockets was deployed in action in July 1941, just weeks after the German invasion began. The *Katyusha* was not a precision weapon, but precision was not really necessary when a battery of rocket launchers, each containing 16 rockets fired into a small area, dropping more than 2,400kg (5,280lb) of explosive onto the target.

A second view of the troops from the 62nd Army liberating a village. At the time this photo was taken, the 62nd Army was penned into a salient and had to take the full brunt of the attack from Paulus' main body, drawn up at the western rim of Stalingrad. What worried Stalin at this stage of the battle was that the 62nd Army was the only combat force left to prevent more than two hundred thousand invaders from entering and capturing the city of Stalingrad.

In what may be a staged photograph, Russian troops employ various weapons from submachine guns to field artillery to repel the advancing Germans.

Russian soldiers willing to defend their homeland at all costs try to prevent the advance of the enemy into the Stalingrad area. These Red Army troops have been deployed to "hold or die". They are all armed with the familiar standard-issue 7.62mm Mosin Nagant M1891/30 bolt-action rifle. These weapons were particularly useful with frontline soldiers and would become widely used by snipers in the ruins of Stalingrad.

Red Army troops are shown during intensive action northwest of Stalingrad. The soldiers all appear to be armed with the 7.62mm Pistolet Pulemet Degtyareva o1940G, or PPD1940 submachine gun. This reliable and effective weapon had a 71-round drum magazine and a cyclic rate of fire of 800 rpm. These weapons were replaced with the PPSh-41 submachine gun. Note that all the troops are wearing *pilotka* sidecaps.

Two Pulemet Degtyareva Pekhotnii (DP) light machine gunners take up a position near to the German front lines northwest of Stalingrad. The DP light machine gun fired a 47-round magazine. This simple gas-operated weapon was used widely by partisans.

Under pulverizing German artillery bombardment, infantry from the 64th Army pull back after suffering high casualties. The soldiers are carrying M1891/30 Mosin Nagant rifles, and one infantryman appears to be armed with a PPSh-41 submachine gun. Note their ankle boots. Not issued socks, the soldiers wrap their legs in puttees made from cloth from worn-out uniforms.

A Red Army gun crew prepares to fire a 122mm M1939 howitzer toward the distant German army.

A scouting section is seen reconnoitring a populated area on the outskirt of Stalingrad. They appear to be wrapped in German camouflage *zeltbahn* and capes. Not only did the *zeltbahn* and waterproof capes help to keep the soldiers well camouflaged, it would also enable them to remain relatively dry in the autumn rains that were rapidly approaching.

Troops move into action northwest of the city in what appears to be a non-posed Soviet propaganda photograph. All the men carry the familiar PPSh-41 submachine gun and wear the basic Soviet kit used by soldiers during the summer. Some of them have slung their rolled ground sheets over their shoulder. Note the understrength five-man gun crew loading a 76.2mm Field Gun Model 1939. The gun had a maximum range of 13.29km (8.25 miles) and fired a 14-lb shell.

A couple of Soviet soldiers, one with a PPSh-41 submachine gun and the other with a PTRS M1941 anti-tank gun, prepare to fire their weapons.

Red Army troops creep along communication trenches with ammunition boxes. On 5 September, with the enemy now no more than two miles from the outskirts of Stalingrad, Stalin himself brutally ordered the launching of "human wave" assaults, which were intended to storm the left flank of the German corridor. From dugouts and a string of trenches, Red Army troops crossed "no man's land" and slammed into enemy formations.

Sappers, one armed with a PPSh-41 submachine gun and the other carrying a mine detector, inch their way over a field in a deadly hunt for anti-tank mines.

Russian troops stay low as they advance. Most of them are wearing the loose-fitting, blouse-like *gymnastiorka* uniform.

A battery of 152mm (5.98in) howitzers delivers a heavy, concentrated barrage on German positions north of Stalingrad. These big guns were more than capable of firing 40kg (88lb) high explosive shells or a 51kg (112lb) semi-armor-piercing shells with a muzzle velocity of 432m/s (472yds/sec). Each gun had a crew of seven. Working hard together, they could easily fire three or four rounds every minute.

Soviet soldiers under fire near the Stalingrad area. The regular spacing of the soldiers suggests that this photograph, like many action photos taken by the Russians during World War Two, was in fact a staged picture. The photographer, who has not taken cover, would have been risking his life if this were a real attack.

A good close-up view of the kit and weapon issued to Russian soldiers. This soldier carries the 7.62mm Mosin Nagant M1891/30 bolt-action rifle. On his back is visible the rolled greatcoat and an attached mess tin. Soviet soldiers preferred German mess tins over their own aluminium pots. Other parts of his basic kit included a greatcoat or blanket, haversack, and an entrenching tool.

Russian sappers were kept busy removing and collecting German anti-tank mines.

Anti-tank gunners move their 45mm Model 1932 L/46 gun into action in the Stalingrad sector. Both anti-tank and heavy Russian artillery immediately laid barrages in front of the most advanced defensive positions, thus furnishing them with a screen of fire that would protect them from attacking enemy infantry and armor. Heavy concentration of artillery fire was very effective against tank assembly points on the Stalingrad Front.

An interesting photograph showing a group of soldiers, two of which are armed with the 14.5mm PTRS M1941 anti-tank gun. The soldiers stoop low as they clamber into the trench. The trench has been dug with the bulk of the dug-up soil thrown towards the enemy positions. The golden rule of digging trenches was "two spade loads of soil towards the enemy, and one to the rear."

Armed with PPSh-41 submachine guns, two steel-helmeted Soviet soldiers pose for the camera using a derelict truck as cover. Although these weapons were not used for sniping, they were very effective at eliminating partially concealed targets at short range. Once their target was deemed neutralized, Soviet submachine gunners would move forward, racing hunched towards the smoke and dust that enveloped a knocked-out German position.

A group of anti-tank gunners covers the advance of attacking Soviet infantry in the vicinity of Kalach. The weapon they are using is a 45mm Model 1932 L/46 gun. This particular model, which was based on the German 3.7cm Rheinmetall PaK 35/36, weighed 510kg (1124lbs) in action and fired a 1.43kg (3.15lb) shell that was capable of easily penetrating 38mm (1.50in) of armor at an angle of 30 degrees at a range of 1000m (1094yd). A very effective anti-tank gun, it remained in service until the end of the war.

Russian men who were conscripted into the defense of Stalingrad man a captured German 3.7cm flak gun. Weapons like these were used in a dual role and were particularly effective against enemy aircraft. Weighing some 1,757kg (3,858lb) and mounted on a cruciform platform, the gun fired a 0.56kg (1.2lb) shell to a vertical height of 4785m (5,235yds) or 6,492m (7,100yds) against ground targets.

Soldiers of the 62nd Army take time to enjoy a much-needed respite and eat a hot meal from a field kitchen. The food is probably *kasha*, a buckwheat porridge that was flavored with either vegetables or meat, depending on what was available to the men at the time. Note the Soviet 7.62mm DP light machine-gun perched on a rock.

Cossack cavalry troops, whose traditional fighting qualities helped them while combating strong enemy efforts in the Stalingrad area, advance along a mountain road. They are wearing their traditional black fleece caps or *papakha*. With their brutal tactics and capability to travel long distances over some of the most inhospitable terrain, the Cossack cavalry could harass retreating enemy infantry with great success. By 22 November, the day Operation "Uranus" began, a 150-mile gap had been ripped open between the German troops on the southern side of the Stalingrad *Kessel* (trapped and isolated pockets known as the "cauldron" or *Kessel*) and Heeresgruppe A down in the Caucasus. It was here in these mountains and hills that the Cossacks would reap their revenge on General Erich von Manstein's army, whose objective was to relieve Paulus' 6.Armee trapped inside the ravaged city.

Two Soviet soldiers rock climb during an operation in an attempt to secure more strategic positions. Both wear *shapka-ushanka* winter caps and carry PPSh-41 submachine guns.

Russian soldiers of the 51st Army positioned south of Stalingrad fight in the Caucasus.

# Soviet Anti-tank Team 1942

In 1941, the Soviet Army began to provide anti-tank rifle units to their formations. Rifle battalions received a platoon of six weapons while motor rifle regiments got a full company with 24 PTRS or PTRD 14.5mm anti-tank rifles. Despite decreased effectiveness on the increasingly thick armor of German panzers, the Red Army fielded these anti-tank rifles until the end of the war.

The PTRD weighed 38 pounds while the PTRS was a hefty 46 pounds. The latter could be broken down into barrel and receiver groups to make more manageable loads. The PTRD was a single shot weapon but the PTRS had a clip loaded five round magazine. Ammunition for either was generally carried in a shoulder bag.

The M1935 pattern field uniform was made in cotton material for summer (as depicted) and wool for winter versions with the latter tending to be a darker shade. The blouse (*gymnastiorka*) was a simple pullover item with a fall collar. The collar patch on which rank insignia was displayed was often not worn by ordinary privates. Prior to 1941, these collar patches were issued in the color of the arm of service (i.e. raspberry red for infantry). The trousers (*sharovari*) were flared similar to riding breeches and were either tucked into tall boots or secured by putties wrapped over top of ankle boots. While the M1940 helmet was the intended headgear in action, the field cap (*pilotka*) was commonly worn in preference.

Field equipment was sparse when compared to the western allies. A variety of belts were issued to carry ammunition pouches and water bottles. Most Soviet soldiers carried a gasmask haversack, although often this carried provisions rather than its intended contents. A simple backpack (*meshok*) was quite commonly carried. It was little more than a drawstring canvas bag with shoulder straps attached. Personal items could also be rolled up in the rain cape (*plashch-palatka*) and be worn across the torso.

VOLSTAD 95

# Red Army Scout Detachment 1942

The *razvedchiki* or reconnaissance units were considered the elite of the Red Army in WWII. Drawn from the best troops in a division, most rifle regiments would have a company of scouts while the division itself had a battalion.

Camouflage clothing was generally unique to scout and sniper units, however engineers, airborne forces and some NKVD reconnaissance troops also wore them. The most recognizable camouflage was the "amoeba" pattern. Dating from 1937-38, this pattern was produced in several shades of dark brown or black printed on green or khaki/tan background. Several types of garments were produced but the most common seems to be the two-piece type worn here. It was a very loose fitting cotton item with a large hood and it was intended to be worn over the issue field uniform. Often, the smock was worn tucked into the trousers. A simple one-piece hooded cape affair was also made from this pattern.

Period photos indicate that Soviet scouts operated with minimal equipment. Items such as binoculars were often captured from their German opponents. Other than ammunition for their weapons, it could be assumed that a water bottle would be carried.

Typically, Red Army scouts were armed with automatic weapons such as the PPSh-41. It wasn't unusual to carry a captured MP40 instead. The sniper on the left is armed with the M1891/30 with a PU scope while the female sniper uses the same rifle fitted with a PE scope. Eight women snipers and two scouts were recipients of the "Hero of the Soviet Union".

VOLSTAD 97

# Junior Sergeant, Rifle Regiment 1942-43

While efforts were made to equip the Red Army soldiers with more practical winter clothing, the wool greatcoat remained very much in use until the end of the war. His rank of junior sergeant is indicated by the enameled triangle worn on the subdued collar patches. Beneath his overcoat would be worn the winter issue wool M1935 uniform. When weather dictated, the *ushanka* winter cap could be worn beneath the M1940 helmet although the fit was somewhat clumsy.

It has been said that the SVT40 automatic rifle was issued primarily to NCO's however recent photographic evidence shows that this weapon had much wider usage. Apparently it was vulnerable to dirt and dust thus it required more care than the much more common bolt action rifles. Spare magazines were carried in a leather pouch on the right of his belt while a canvas pouch on the other side carried three F-1 fragmentation grenades. A gasmask bag is slung over the right shoulder.

VOLSTAD '03

# Private, Motor Rifle Regiment 1942-43

The quilted winter jacket (*telogreika*) was a practical garment for winter combat, particularly for troops being transported on tanks. Despite their title, Motor Rifles were constantly short of motor transport and instead, rode T-34's into action as *tankoviy desant*, dismounting to fight on foot when appropriate.

Early versions of the *telogreika* had a fall collar, but photos from Stalingrad show the "stand" collar already in use. Matching padded trousers were produced but not always available, leaving winter weight *sharovari* trousers to suffice. Typical calf length boots are worn. It may be interesting to note that the shaft of many such boot was made of painted tarpaulin material rather than leather. The issuing of proper felt winter boots seems to have been reserved for the harshest weather.

During the winter of 1941, the gray *shapka-ushanka* winter hat was first issued. Officer's versions used real fur but the enlisted men's variant used synthetic pile nicknamed "fish fur". Generally, but not always, the "red star" was worn centered on the front flap.

Typically, equipment is minimal. The web and leather belt supports his spare drum for the PPSh-41 and a grenade pouch for RGD-33 grenades. A scrounged SVT40 bayonet has also been slipped on the belt. The shoulder straps indicate that the *meshok* rucksack is worn on his back.

VOLSTAD '03

These are some of the troops who fought against General von Manstein's relief expedition to Stalingrad on 12 December 1942.

These Russian soldiers are armed with a variety of weapons that include Mosin Nagant M1891/30 bolt action rifles and Pulemet Degtyareva Pekhotnii (DP) light machineguns.

A Red Army scout keeps watch from a tree somewhere on the front lines along the Stalingrad Front as the German offensive gathers momentum. He is wearing a British greatcoat and is armed with a PPSh-41 submachine gun.

Crewmembers of a Soviet 82-PM 36 82mm mortar positioned near Stalingrad await the order to fire, which appears to be a hand signal from their commander. All three men are wearing the *shapka-ushanka* fur winter cap, which was widely worn throughout the Red Army during the winter months.

Soldiers attempt to push forward during intensive fighting northwest of Stalingrad. In Russia, the seasons change dramatically. All the soldiers are wearing heavy greatcoats provided by the British as part of their aid to the Soviet Union. The soldiers called these garments "a present from the King of England."

A US-supplied $\frac{1}{4}$-ton 4x4 Willys MA Jeep tows a Soviet anti-tank gun on the outskirts of Stalingrad. The advance of the Red Army was not normally conducted by vehicle. More often the troops traveled on horseback, on the engine deck of tanks and assault vehicles, in captured vehicles, and on foot. Although the US Jeep was unable to carry many passengers, the troops tried to cram an entire anti-tank crew on board this one.

A soldier prepares to fire a Maxim 1910 machine gun during combat on the outskirts of Stalingrad. The gun was far from easy to maneuver, even on its wheeled Sokolov mount. The heavy shield added to the gunner's misery every time he needed to move it to a different position. But the Maxim did not prove a problem in Stalingrad since it was used solely as a defensive weapon and did not need to be laboriously hauled from one position to another. However, following the Russian victory at Stalingrad, the machine gun was used more often in offensive roles, and the heavy shield was subsequently removed to reduce its weight.

A battery of field guns stands ready to defend against the German attempt to capture Stalingrad.

The overcoats and fur caps worn by these artillerymen indicate that winter has set in. Winter weather would make the horrible fight for Stalingrad even more nightmarish.

The vigilant crewmembers of an 45mm Model 1932 L/46 anti-tank gun wait for their time in combat to arrive.

Signalmen of the 35th Guards Division lay a field telephone wire among the ruins inside the city. This photograph was probably taken on the southern fringe of the city during October 1942. The once great 35th Guards Division now totalled some 250 soldiers. Normally, 10,000 soldiers were listed in one single division. This was a clear indication of the enormity of losses sustained by the Red Army during this period of fighting.

Red Army troops wearing Model 1940 steel helmets charge through the ruins of Stalingrad. Rushes like this were a common Soviet infantry tactic. Although it generally caused high casualties, the tactic frequently unbalanced the enemy and drove them from their defensive positions in chaotic disorder.

Tank-riding troops move forward to close on German positions. This was another common Soviet tactic that required infantry to destroy enemy anti-tank guns before tanks made the breakthrough. When tanks approached close to a German position, the tank riders would dismount and run ahead of the tanks, cheering and yelling as they ran into the rain of enemy bullets. Despite the fact that they could result in hundreds of dead and wounded soldiers, the tactics employed were often successful.

A soldier aims a 14.5mm PTRS M1941, an automatic anti-tank gun with five cartridges, on the bank of the Volga. The weapon was so effective it was frequently used in a dual role and could shoot down low-flying enemy aircraft. Of particular interest is the soldier to the gunner's right, the so-called charge man, who is holding a 14.5mm cartridge BS-41.

Rubble-strewn streets in the *Kessel* part of Stalingrad. The city suffered terrible bombing raids during the beginning of the battle in late August 1942, which killed more than 40,000 of the city's inhabitants.

Russian POWs are marched westward to a grim fate as slave laborers, or worse, to end their life in a concentration camp.

In the headquarters of the 13th Guards Rifle Division of General Rodimtsev, Russian commanders consult maps and discuss the deployment of troops in the Stalingrad area. By late November, General Zhukov had moved 134 divisions across the Don. Their tanks had turned westward, probing into the straggling elements of the German rear. Their infantry had turned east to build an iron ring around Stalingrad. Zhukov ordered his commanders to keep the whole pocket under heavy bombardment from his big guns on the east bank of the Volga.

Russian soldiers advance to begin one of the street battles in Stalingrad. Many soldiers preferred to stumble through the ruins since movement on foot over exposed areas of ground in a large city street could be lethal. Some German hit squads or snipers roamed the city and killed a great number of soldiers, especially in relatively open areas.

A Russian infantry gun opens fire on enemy positions just inside the *Kessel* perimeter. This M1942 ZIS-3 76mm gun normally had a gun crew of six or seven men, which would provide the maximum rate of fire. The gun, which was mounted on a 57mm carriage, could fire a range of high explosive and armor piercing ammunition. The maximum range with explosive was 13.29km (8.25 miles). This was considered more than enough distance during urban combat.

A group of riflemen storms a suspected enemy position as parts of Paulus' 6.Army begin to penetrate the outskirts of the city. Lightning attacks like this were commonly seen among the fighting techniques of the Russians. They were experts in urban fighting and enjoyed great success defending a number of areas inside the blitzed city.

Red Army soldiers move forward across "no man's land" following a successful raid against a German defensive position inside Stalingrad. Casualties increased when they reached the congested, bombed-out avenues of the city.

The crew of a Red Army trench mortar dislodges an enemy unit from a strongpoint on the outskirts of the city. They are using an 82-PM 36 82mm mortar. This weapon could fire a 3.35kg (7.39lb) bomb to a maximum range of 3000m (3,279yd). It could also fire German 81mm ammunition, though with much less accuracy.

A mortar crew fires salvoes at enemy positions from inside the burning wreckage of the *Krasnity Octiabar* (Red October) factory complex. The factory was defended fanatically by the 13th Guards Division. Along with the Tractor and Barrikady factories to the north, the Red October complex would be the key to the defensive position of Stalingrad and would prevent 6.Armee from escaping across the Volga.

Soviet workers fight for their plant in Stalingrad's factory area, where Red Army soldiers were blockading enemy defensive positions. They are both armed with M1891/30 rifles. One of the workers has a bayonet attached to his rifle, which gives a clear indication of the close combat that often resulted in hand-to-hand duels with the enemy.

In November 1942, soldiers take up a new defensive line inside the ruins of a factory building. Cautiously the soldiers work their way forward through the rubble. The wreckage of the buildings, which blocked access to roads, was a constant hindrance to the movement of armor. But the rubble helped the Russians conceal and protect fortified bunkers and cellars. Later in the battle the Germans themselves employed the same tactic and began to blow up buildings as they retreated, just to create fortified positions.

Street fighting inside Stalingrad. Red Army soldiers attempt to dislodge enemy troops that have fortified themselves in a house.

The picture is one of a series taken in the destroyed streets of Stalingrad and shows Soviet soldiers preparing to move forward following days of bitter fighting. The enemy troops who had to endure this kind of urban battle later recalled it as "Germany's World War II Verdun."

Russian soldiers torch a building, setting it ablaze while Germans are still inside. Outside the burning house, the crew of a Soviet anti-tank gun moves forward to intercept enemy tanks that have been spotted moving forward.

Advancing slowly with rifles at the ready, soldiers from the 62nd Army push through into the *Kessel* perimeter. The Germans trapped inside the *Kessel* were at least twenty-five miles from the nearest friendly troops. By now, seven Soviet armies were holding 6.Armee in a hostile embrace. The 21st and 65th Armies pushed through to the north, while the 57th and 24th Armies prevented the Germans from exiting to the west and the east. The 66th and 64th pushed up from the south, while the 62nd Army held the Volga shoreline in Stalingrad itself.

Two Red Army snipers practice their deadly skill within the factory complex of the city. One is armed with the Tokarev SVT1940 automatic rifle fitted with a 3.5 PV telescopic sight. This rifle, which was perfect weapon for hunting down an elusive enemy hiding within the ruins, could easily pick off the unwary.

Two Red Army soldiers dressed in British greatcoats patrol inside the *Kessel*. Although these greatcoats provided adequate warmth, there were still deficiencies in winter clothing among many of the Russian troops fighting in and around Stalingrad. During early December, following the success of Operation "Uranus", nearly every soldier received rabbit fur gloves, sheepskin jerkins, quilted jackets, and a gray fur *ushanka*.

This photograph provides a good example of the total destruction of Stalingrad that resulted from the prolonged combat in and around the city.

The devastating bombing and fighting turned many acres of the city of Stalingrad, including stretches of the Volga shore, into a desolate wasteland of death.

Steel-helmeted Soviet soldiers participate in the brutal fighting in the heart of the city. The soldiers are all wearing the basic kit of a Red Army soldier. The troops appear to have launched a sudden, violent attack against enemy positions, which was a traditional tactic employed by the Russians when the enemy was considered to be weakening in strength.

Red Army soldiers move forward to meet yet another attack during street fighting on the outskirts of the city. Movement on foot across the exposed ground of a large city could be lethal during combat, so sewers were used, or trenches were dug, to enable infantry to safely move from one building to another. Frequently infantry rushes like this across "no man's land" resulted in the total destruction of entire units.

38

North of Stalingrad soldiers of the Soviet 65th Army run to take cover from the bullets of a well-positioned German machine-gun nest. All the soldiers are warmly dressed in winter clothing, including *shapka-ushanka* caps and rabbit fur gloves. Judging by the stocky appearance of the men, they are probably also wearing padded quilted jackets under their greatcoats.

Dressed warmly, the crew of a Model 1932 L/46 anti-tank gun stoically awaits their chance to combat the renowned German *panzers*. Note that horses are used to haul the caisson.

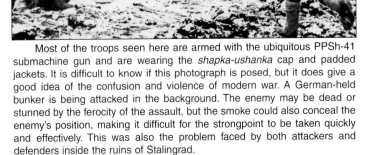

Another photograph taken north of Stalingrad shows Soviet troops advancing toward a German defensive position. The Russians were masters at winter combat and showed remarkable skill and tenacity at taking out enemy defenses. But as the battle of Stalingrad continued, the Germans gained experience combating Russian defensive tactics and became more difficult to neutralize.

Most of the troops seen here are armed with the ubiquitous PPSh-41 submachine gun and are wearing the *shapka-ushanka* cap and padded jackets. It is difficult to know if this photograph is posed, but it does give a good idea of the confusion and violence of modern war. A German-held bunker is being attacked in the background. The enemy may be dead or stunned by the ferocity of the assault, but the smoke could also conceal the enemy's position, making it difficult for the strongpoint to be taken quickly and effectively. This was also the problem faced by both attackers and defenders inside the ruins of Stalingrad.

A battery of Model 1910/30 field howitzers in action. These veteran World War I howitzers were mainly used in the early years of World War II. They were upgraded during the 1930s with solid pneumatic-tired wheels. The gun could fire a 22kg (47.8lb) shell at a maximum range of 8,940m (9,771yd).

A Soviet machine gunner at the Stalingrad battlefront just west of the city is about to open fire with his Maxim M1910 machine gun. The machine gunner is wearing the conventional headgear worn by Soviet tank crews. The particular greatcoat he is wearing offered hardly any protection against the bitter winter chill.

A reconnaissance unit armed with standard Soviet weapons marches through the snow. They are all dressed in short sheepskin coats and have their weapons slung over their shoulders, displaying an unusually relaxed attitude.

Soldiers dressed in two-piece, white camouflage smocks advance through the perimeter of the *Kessel*. Note that the soldier at the far left armed with a PPSh-41 submachine gun has been wrapped his head with a scarf to prevent his head from freezing inside his helmet. Frequently the troops' steel helmets became like freezers and, as a result, they were compelled to insulate either their heads or the helmet itself.

Racing into action northwest of Stalingrad, Red Army troops wearing their distinctive white camouflage smocks press forward against the thinning enemy front lines circling the city. They are armed with DP light machine-guns, PPSh-41 submachine guns, and M1891/30 bolt action rifles.

German soldiers surrender to a group of Red Army troops. Thousands of captured German soldiers on the Stalingrad Front never returned home. They were either starved or worked to death in labor camps, or simply froze to death in open prison camps waiting for transportation east. A number of Russian units were ordered to not even take prisoners.

Dressed in a white camouflage smock with a hood, a sniper armed with a Mosin Nagant Model 1891/30 rifle with a x4 PE telescopic sight, prepares to pick off German stragglers on the Stalingrad Front. Although snipers were used extensively on both sides throughout the war, Stalingrad was the perfect hunting ground for them.

Fighting on the Stalingrad Front in December 1942. Soldiers of the Red Army advance through the snow under the protection of a T-34/76 tank. The Soviet Army had always been experts in winter operations and exploiting severe weather conditions. The T-34 tank was also well suited to the hard, frozen plains. The big road wheels also allowed it to exploit very muddy roads.

Two soldiers wearing sheepskin coats and *shapka-ushanka* caps confer with local peasants following the liberation of their village in early December 1942. These soldiers are well clothed for combat in the freezing temperatures of the Russian steppe. They are probably well fed, too, since food could be demanded from the local population.

Charging into action across the snow, Soviet soldiers carrying Mosin Nagant bolt-action rifles and 14.5mm PTRS M1941 anti-tank guns yell and scream like wild tribesman. Making loud noises in chorus as they went into attack was not only a way of relieving the terrible anxieties caused by rushing enemy lines, it was also a form of intimidation against the enemy. The Soviets used this tactic until the very last days of the war.

Fighting on the steppe on the Stalingrad Front, the 66th Army moves into action while heavier weapons cover its advance through a smoke screen. A number of weapons are at hand during this attack, including the PPSh-41 submachine gun, the M1891/30 rifle, the Maxim 1910 water-cooled machine gun, and the Pulemet Degtyareva Pekhotnii (DP) light machinegun. This DP weapon fired ammunition from a 47-round drum magazine at 520 to 580 rounds a minute.

Armed with PPSh-41 submachine guns, three soldiers open fire on the outskirts of the *Kessel* perimeter. The short range of these submachine guns ensured that the troops launched their attacks with noticeable success. Beneath their snow camouflage the men would be wearing a padded sheepskin jacket, padded trousers and a fleece cap. Although the clothing they wore was basic, it was very effective in extreme weather conditions.

Red Army troops in action dressed in white camouflage smocks. Soviet soldiers armed with submachine guns and rifles developed a clever technique of crawling toward enemy lines while dragging their weapons beside them.

Once the Russian troops had crawled close enough to the German defenses their commander would scream out to attack, and the soldiers would pick themselves up from the snow and begin charging, howling and cheering as they advanced.

Steel-helmeted soldiers from the 57th Army, who were preventing 6.Armee from escaping east of Stalingrad, charge German-held positions with M1891/30 rifles. By not wearing white camouflage smocks, these men became easy targets for enemy snipers and machine gun posts. Further, German aircraft could easily identify Russian soldiers dressed in their regular uniforms advancing across the plain.

Two Soviet sappers remove enemy mines from a snow-covered village street northwest of Stalingrad. Both sappers are armed with PPSh-41 submachine guns. They are dressed in greatcoats and wear the synthetic fur pile or felt *ushanka* cap.

The Germans laid hundreds of thousands of mines along the Stalingrad Front that consequently posed a constant problem to the movement of the Soviet Army.

This photograph, which was taken outside the village near a lake, shows more sappers removing mines from a road.

More sappers clear mines from a position in front of a village. The most common and most cost effective German anti-tank mine was the Teller-Mine (TMi). It came in several variants, the earliest being the TMi 29, which was used during the 1930s. The TMi29 was replaced with the TMi 35 at the start of the war, but it continued to see widespread service until 1943. Because the German anti-tank mines were so well constructed, Russian soldiers were able to remove them and use them against the Germans themselves.

Just outside Stalingrad in December 1942, Red Army anti-tank riflemen advance to new firing positions to fight a group of well-entrenched armored vehicles. They are hauling PTRS M1941 anti-tank guns.

These men may have been attached to a Punishment Battalion since they are not wearing camouflage clothing. Punishment Battalion troops were ordered to dress in their standard uniforms in order to draw enemy fire, so that the enemy could be easily located.

Troops in the Punishment Battalions often fought with no prospect of survival and were used by Russian commanders as cannon fodder on the front lines. The casualty rate among soldiers of the Punishment Battalions can only be imagined.

Dismounted cavalry armed with M1891/30 rifles fire at low-flying Ju52 transport planes that are attempting to drop supplies to Paulus' trapped 6.Armee. With a muzzle velocity of 811m, this weapon was more than capable of hitting slow low-flying aircraft. Although outdated, the weapon was an extremely effective and accurate rifle.

Russian troops storm shattered German positions on the Stalingrad Front. Trench mortar gunners can be seen supporting the advancing infantry. Their weapon is a 50-PM 38 mortar. In the snow, however, the effectiveness of the mortar was sometimes reduced considerably by the base plate settling on the snow at a slight angle.

Red Army scouts move forward through a forest just north of Stalingrad. The commander orders his men to halt and wait before continuing on. They are all wearing snow camouflage suits and probably are all armed with M1891/30 rifles. Another popular weapon used in some of the most extremely harsh terrain was the SVT1940 automatic rifle, which had a 20-round magazine.

A Soviet machine gun unit crawls toward a German position that has already received a battering from aerial attacks. The two soldiers in the lead painstakingly drag a heavy Maxim 1910 water-cooled machine gun through the snow. The wheeled Sokolov mount, along with its shield, weighed some 74kg (163lb).

Troops north of Stalingrad make their way out of a forest clearing in January 1943. The soldiers are warmly dressed in sheepskin coats and *shapka-ushanka* caps. Although the winter was harsh, the long, drawn out hours of darkness provided excellent cover for groups of soldiers hoping to avoid being attacked. Note that the soldier at the rear of the column is carrying a mine detector.

Accompanied by two T-34/76 tanks, soldiers clad in white camouflage suits advance warily through a bleak winter landscape during the fighting for Stalingrad.

After the infantry had successfully knocked out enemy anti-tank guns, the T-34/76 tanks were brought up to help destroy the remaining German positions. Attached to the soldiers' Mosin Nagant M1891/30 rifles are hinged-spiked bayonets that could fold back behind the barrel of the gun. This is evidence of the close quarter fighting that raged within Stalingrad. Hand-to-hand fighting was a common occurrence, especially when each side fought desperately to the death in an attempt to hold on to a position.

Red Army soldiers storm an abandoned German airstrip near Stalingrad and capture a number of Focke Wulf aircraft. A few of the aircraft have already sustained serious damage, probably caused by heavy artillery. The Soviet soldiers considered the capture of airfields with aircraft a worthy victory. It not only prevented the Germans from supplying its dwindling forces, but it also enabled the Russians to employ the airfield for their own use. On occasion, large German planes became temporary homes for Soviet families living near abandoned airfields.

Soviet soldiers run through a snow-covered town. Wearing their distinctive greatcoats, fur caps and ankle boots, the troops appear to be embroiled in combat. However, this could be another posed photo. The dead soldier seems to have been strategically placed to complete the picture. Both sides were adept at using propaganda to support their cause. But faked Soviet victories now represented the reality of the battlefield, unlike earlier propaganda photographs.

Soviet soldiers fight their way inch by inch through a factory building. They are armed with a motley collection of arms including PPSh-41 submachine guns, M1891/30 rifles, and at least one pistol. A number of "combat" pictures taken by Soviet Army photographers were posed. Evidence suggests that this is a staged photograph. An operation as hazardous as this would probably be conducted at night. Further, judging by the position of the photographer, he would have surely been a prime target for a sniper. Snipers were a constant worry for both sides, especially inside factories. The Russians had no doubt already taken this factory.

Soviet troops stumble forward into battle over piles of rubble. A number of Russian soldiers began reporting in mid-January that they had shot and killed German soldiers who were risking their lives by venturing into "no man's land" to look for food on the bodies of dead Red Army soldiers. It became apparent by January 1943 that the soldiers of Paulus' once great 6.Armee were starving to death.

A Russian soldier killed in the fighting just inside the *Kessel*, where the process of attrition was born, has become part of the battlefield debris. Despite the many Soviet losses, the Red Army soldiers who engaged in the countless murderous skirmishes knew they were much better suited for urban combat than was their foe.

These beleaguered German soldiers are part of the final surrender of Paulus' 6.Armee at Stalingrad in early February 1943. From the appearance of these troops, the Germans had not received proper winter clothing. The inadequate supply of winter gear forced the German troops to improvise with varying degrees of success. Many of them wear Soviet clothing that was taken from corpses beneath their uniforms. These consist of baggy quilted trousers, buttonless tunic shirts and quilted jackets.

Because of the freezing temperatures, many of the German soldiers discarded their steel helmets, which had become virtual freezer compartments, and now wear scarves, and even Russian foot bandages, wrapped around their heads to keep out the terrible cold.

Several of the German prisoners-of-war are wearing captured Russian mittens. In a desperate attempt to keep warm, some soldiers resorted to killing stray dogs in order to skin them for fur gloves. Some soldiers even tried to skin dead horses to make crude tunics, which often turned out to be uncomfortable and ill fitting.

This picture of stoic defeat shows Paulus, promoted to Field-Marshal on 31 January 1943, still wearing his uniform after his surrender. Following his capture, Paulus was driven in his own staff car from 64th Army headquarters to the Don Front headquarters outside Zavarykino, some fifty or so miles from Stalingrad, to be questioned. Captain Dyatlenko of the NKVD, Captain Voronev, General Rokossovsky, and General Telegin were the first to interview Paulus. To their surprise, they discovered they had captured the greatest prize of the war so far, a Field-Marshal.

Dressed in a combination of German- and Russian-issue uniform parts, German soldiers from Paulus' 6.Armee are led away past a shell-riddled building to face an uncertain fate as POWs.

Soviet soldiers march through Stalingrad for the first time in five months without the prospect or worry of being attacked. But with the enemy now expelled from the city, on 2 February Zhukov finally unleashed the long-awaited Voronezh Front (codenamed Operation "Star"). These soldiers, after fighting continuously for months, would soon see action in the southwest toward Kharkov. Victory was now beckoning to them.